M000168662

DAILY
TO-DO LIST
NOTEBOOK

INDEPENDENTLY PUBLISHED BY

PAPIER BLACK

BASIC PRODUCTIVITY NOTEBOOKS

ISBN: 9781790374694

IF FOUND, PLEASE RETURN TO:

BRAIN DUMP

Use this page as task triage. Write down ALL tasks rattling around in your brain and assign them a priority and a date. Transfer these tasks to your future pages as necessary then cross them out.

Tasks	PRIORITY (HIGH, MEDIUM, LOW)			ASSIGN A DATE
BD: HIGH PROFILE SPEAKERS!	●	○	○	2/12
Biotech Primer Acquisition	○	●	○	
	○	○	○	
	○	○	○	
	○	○	○	
	○	○	○	
	○	○	○	
	○	○	○	
	○	○	○	
	○	○	○	
	○	○	○	
	○	○	○	
	○	○	○	
	○	○	○	
	○	○	○	
	○	○	○	
	○	○	○	
	○	○	○	
	○	○	○	
	○	○	○	
	○	○	○	
	○	○	○	
	○	○	○	

3 Most Important Tasks

	DUE	DONE
- Budget for MVS		✓
- Keynotes		☐
— EPO Letter		✓

Other Tasks

	DUE	DONE
- Budget Contracts		☐
- Gap analysis		☐
- IPCC Webinar overview		☐
- Overall webinar overview		☐
- Jocelyn - Budget $		☐
- Patrik - offering virtual valuation		☐
- TBD Panel - Astellas ✗		☐
- Jazz - Send moderator ideas		☐
		☐
		☐
		☐
		☐
		☐

NOTES

Melissa: ✗Reviews/titles←
 ✗ - webinars - budget
 ✗ - Meeting w/ Bernie - education
 ✗ - morale
 ✗ - Keynotes

3 Most Important Tasks

DUE   D ONE

....	~~fire song~~	☐
....		☐
....		☐

Other Tasks

DUE   DONE

....	fire song	☒
....	Can MO	☒
....	Vlog	☒
....	Drive	☒
....	ing DAYs	☒
....	to fire	☐
....	C ATZNEY	☐
....		☐
....		☐
....		☐
....		☐
....		☐
....		☐

NOTES

DAY: M T W Th F S Su   DATE: _____ / _____ / _____

3 Most Important Tasks

DUE   DONE

....

....

....

Other Tasks

DUE   DONE

....

....

....

....

....

....

....

....

....

....

....

....

....

NOTES

DAY: M T W Th F S Su   DATE: _____/_____/_____

3 Most Important Tasks

	DUE	DONE
....		
....		
....		

Other Tasks

	DUE	DONE
....		
....		
....		
....		
....		
....		
....		
....		
....		
....		
....		
....		
....		

NOTES

3 Most Important Tasks

DUE   DONE

....

....

....

Other Tasks

DUE   DONE

....

....

....

....

....

....

....

....

....

....

....

....

....

NOTES

DAY: M T W Th F S Su   DATE: _____ / _____ / _____

3 Most Important Tasks

DUE   DONE

.... [   ] [ ]

.... [   ] [ ]

.... [   ] [ ]

Other Tasks

DUE   DONE

.... [   ] [ ]

.... [   ] [ ]

.... [   ] [ ]

.... [   ] [ ]

.... [   ] [ ]

.... [   ] [ ]

.... [   ] [ ]

.... [   ] [ ]

.... [   ] [ ]

.... [   ] [ ]

.... [   ] [ ]

.... [   ] [ ]

.... [   ] [ ]

NOTES

DAY: M T W Th F S Su   DATE: _____ / _____ / _____

3 Most Important Tasks

DUE   DONE

.... [ ] [ ]

.... [ ] [ ]

.... [ ] [ ]

Other Tasks

DUE   DONE

.... [ ] [ ]

.... [ ] [ ]

.... [ ] [ ]

.... [ ] [ ]

.... [ ] [ ]

.... [ ] [ ]

.... [ ] [ ]

.... [ ] [ ]

.... [ ] [ ]

.... [ ] [ ]

.... [ ] [ ]

.... [ ] [ ]

.... [ ] [ ]

NOTES

BRAIN DUMP

Use this page as task triage. Write down ALL tasks rattling around in your brain and assign them a priority and a date. Transfer these tasks to your future pages as necessary then cross them out.

Tasks	PRIORITY (HIGH, MEDIUM, LOW)			ASSIGN A DATE
....	◯	◯	◯	▭
....	◯	◯	◯	▭
....	◯	◯	◯	▭
....	◯	◯	◯	▭
....	◯	◯	◯	▭
....	◯	◯	◯	▭
....	◯	◯	◯	▭
....	◯	◯	◯	▭
....	◯	◯	◯	▭
....	◯	◯	◯	▭
....	◯	◯	◯	▭
....	◯	◯	◯	▭
....	◯	◯	◯	▭
....	◯	◯	◯	▭
....	◯	◯	◯	▭
....	◯	◯	◯	▭
....	◯	◯	◯	▭
....	◯	◯	◯	▭
....	◯	◯	◯	▭
....	◯	◯	◯	▭
....	◯	◯	◯	▭
....	◯	◯	◯	▭
....	◯	◯	◯	▭
....	◯	◯	◯	▭

3 Most Important Tasks

	DUE	DONE
....		☐
....		☐
....		☐

Other Tasks

	DUE	DONE
....		☐
....		☐
....		☐
....		☐
....		☐
....		☐
....		☐
....		☐
....		☐
....		☐
....		☐
....		☐
....		☐

NOTES

3 Most Important Tasks

DUE   DONE

....

....

....

Other Tasks

DUE   DONE

....

....

....

....

....

....

....

....

....

....

....

....

....

NOTES

3 Most Important Tasks

DUE   DONE

.... ▭ ☐

.... ▭ ☐

.... ▭ ☐

Other Tasks

DUE   DONE

.... ▭ ☐

.... ▭ ☐

.... ▭ ☐

.... ▭ ☐

.... ▭ ☐

.... ▭ ☐

.... ▭ ☐

.... ▭ ☐

.... ▭ ☐

.... ▭ ☐

.... ▭ ☐

.... ▭ ☐

.... ▭ ☐

NOTES

DAY: M T W Th F S Su   DATE: _____ / _____ / _____

3 Most Important Tasks

	DUE	DONE
....	☐	☐
....	☐	☐
....	☐	☐

Other Tasks

	DUE	DONE
....	☐	☐
....	☐	☐
....	☐	☐
....	☐	☐
....	☐	☐
....	☐	☐
....	☐	☐
....	☐	☐
....	☐	☐
....	☐	☐
....	☐	☐
....	☐	☐
....	☐	☐

NOTES

3 Most Important Tasks

DUE   DONE

....

....

....

Other Tasks

DUE   DONE

....

....

....

....

....

....

....

....

....

....

....

....

....

NOTES

DAY: M T W Th F S Su   DATE: _____ / _____ / _____

3 Most Important Tasks

DUE   DONE

.... [ ] ☐

.... [ ] ☐

.... [ ] ☐

Other Tasks

DUE   DONE

.... [ ] ☐

.... [ ] ☐

.... [ ] ☐

.... [ ] ☐

.... [ ] ☐

.... [ ] ☐

.... [ ] ☐

.... [ ] ☐

.... [ ] ☐

.... [ ] ☐

.... [ ] ☐

.... [ ] ☐

.... [ ] ☐

NOTES

3 Most Important Tasks

DUE   DONE

....

....

....

Other Tasks

DUE   DONE

....

....

....

....

....

....

....

....

....

....

....

....

NOTES

BRAIN DUMP

Use this page as task triage. Write down ALL tasks rattling around in your brain and assign them a priority and a date. Transfer these tasks to your future pages as necessary then cross them out.

Tasks

PRIORITY
(HIGH, MEDIUM, LOW)

ASSIGN A DATE

.... ○ ○ ○ [ ]

.... ○ ○ ○ [ ]

.... ○ ○ ○ [ ]

.... ○ ○ ○ [ ]

.... ○ ○ ○ [ ]

.... ○ ○ ○ [ ]

.... ○ ○ ○ [ ]

.... ○ ○ ○ [ ]

.... ○ ○ ○ [ ]

.... ○ ○ ○ [ ]

.... ○ ○ ○ [ ]

.... ○ ○ ○ [ ]

.... ○ ○ ○ [ ]

.... ○ ○ ○ [ ]

.... ○ ○ ○ [ ]

.... ○ ○ ○ [ ]

.... ○ ○ ○ [ ]

.... ○ ○ ○ [ ]

.... ○ ○ ○ [ ]

.... ○ ○ ○ [ ]

.... ○ ○ ○ [ ]

.... ○ ○ ○ [ ]

.... ○ ○ ○ [ ]

.... ○ ○ ○ [ ]

.... ○ ○ ○ [ ]

3 Most Important Tasks

DUE   DONE

....

....

....

Other Tasks

DUE   DONE

....

....

....

....

....

....

....

....

....

....

....

....

....

NOTES

DAY: M T W Th F S Su   DATE: _____ / _____ / _____

3 Most Important Tasks

	DUE	DONE
....		☐
....		☐
....		☐

Other Tasks

	DUE	DONE
....		☐
....		☐
....		☐
....		☐
....		☐
....		☐
....		☐
....		☐
....		☐
....		☐
....		☐
....		☐
....		☐

NOTES

3 Most Important Tasks

	DUE	DONE
....		
....		
....		

Other Tasks

	DUE	DONE
....		
....		
....		
....		
....		
....		
....		
....		
....		
....		
....		
....		
....		

NOTES

3 Most Important Tasks

DUE   DONE

....

....

....

Other Tasks

DUE   DONE

....

....

....

....

....

....

....

....

....

....

....

....

NOTES

3 Most Important Tasks

DUE   DONE

....

....

....

Other Tasks

DUE   DONE

....

....

....

....

....

....

....

....

....

....

....

....

NOTES

3 Most Important Tasks

DUE   DONE

....

....

....

Other Tasks

DUE   DONE

....

....

....

....

....

....

....

....

....

....

....

....

....

NOTES

3 Most Important Tasks

	DUE	DONE
....	☐	☐
....	☐	☐
....	☐	☐

Other Tasks

	DUE	DONE
....	☐	☐
....	☐	☐
....	☐	☐
....	☐	☐
....	☐	☐
....	☐	☐
....	☐	☐
....	☐	☐
....	☐	☐
....	☐	☐
....	☐	☐
....	☐	☐
....	☐	☐

NOTES

BRAIN DUMP

Use this page as task triage. Write down ALL tasks rattling around in your brain and assign them a priority and a date. Transfer these tasks to your future pages as necessary then cross them out.

Tasks

Tasks	PRIORITY (HIGH, MEDIUM, LOW)	ASSIGN A DATE
....	○ ○ ○	
....	○ ○ ○	
....	○ ○ ○	
....	○ ○ ○	
....	○ ○ ○	
....	○ ○ ○	
....	○ ○ ○	
....	○ ○ ○	
....	○ ○ ○	
....	○ ○ ○	
....	○ ○ ○	
....	○ ○ ○	
....	○ ○ ○	
....	○ ○ ○	
....	○ ○ ○	
....	○ ○ ○	
....	○ ○ ○	
....	○ ○ ○	
....	○ ○ ○	
....	○ ○ ○	
....	○ ○ ○	
....	○ ○ ○	
....	○ ○ ○	
....	○ ○ ○	

3 Most Important Tasks

DUE   DONE

....

....

....

Other Tasks

DUE   DONE

....

....

....

....

....

....

....

....

....

....

....

....

....

NOTES

DAY: M T W Th F S Su   DATE: _____ / _____ / _____

3 Most Important Tasks

DUE   DONE

....

....

....

Other Tasks

DUE   DONE

....

....

....

....

....

....

....

....

....

....

....

....

....

NOTES

3 Most Important Tasks

DUE   DONE

....

....

....

Other Tasks

DUE   DONE

....

....

....

....

....

....

....

....

....

....

....

....

....

NOTES

3 Most Important Tasks

DUE   DONE

....

....

....

Other Tasks

DUE   DONE

....

....

....

....

....

....

....

....

....

....

....

....

NOTES

3 Most Important Tasks

DUE   DONE

....

....

....

Other Tasks

DUE   DONE

....

....

....

....

....

....

....

....

....

....

....

....

....

NOTES

3 Most Important Tasks

DUE   DONE

....

....

....

Other Tasks

DUE   DONE

....

....

....

....

....

....

....

....

....

....

....

....

....

NOTES

3 Most Important Tasks

DUE   DONE

....

....

....

Other Tasks

DUE   DONE

....

....

....

....

....

....

....

....

....

....

....

....

....

NOTES

BRAIN DUMP

Use this page as task triage. Write down ALL tasks rattling around in your brain and assign them a priority and a date. Transfer these tasks to your future pages as necessary then cross them out.

Tasks

PRIORITY
(HIGH, MEDIUM, LOW)

ASSIGN A DATE

3 Most Important Tasks

	DUE	DONE
....		☐
....		☐
....		☐

Other Tasks

	DUE	DONE
....		☐
....		☐
....		☐
....		☐
....		☐
....		☐
....		☐
....		☐
....		☐
....		☐
....		☐
....		☐
....		☐

NOTES

3 Most Important Tasks

DUE   DONE

....

....

....

Other Tasks

DUE   DONE

....

....

....

....

....

....

....

....

....

....

....

....

....

NOTES

3 Most Important Tasks

	DUE	DONE
....		☐
....		☐
....		☐

Other Tasks

	DUE	DONE
....		☐
....		☐
....		☐
....		☐
....		☐
....		☐
....		☐
....		☐
....		☐
....		☐
....		☐
....		☐
....		☐

NOTES

DAY: M   T   W   Th   F   S   Su   DATE: _____ / _____ / _____

3 Most Important Tasks

DUE   DONE

....   [ ]   [ ]

....   [ ]   [ ]

....   [ ]   [ ]

Other Tasks

DUE   DONE

....   [ ]   [ ]

....   [ ]   [ ]

....   [ ]   [ ]

....   [ ]   [ ]

....   [ ]   [ ]

....   [ ]   [ ]

....   [ ]   [ ]

....   [ ]   [ ]

....   [ ]   [ ]

....   [ ]   [ ]

....   [ ]   [ ]

....   [ ]   [ ]

....   [ ]   [ ]

NOTES

DAY: M T W Th F S Su   DATE: _____ / _____ / _____

3 Most Important Tasks

DUE   DONE

....

....

....

Other Tasks

DUE   DONE

....

....

....

....

....

....

....

....

....

....

....

....

....

NOTES

DAY: M T W Th F S Su   DATE: _____ / _____ / _____

3 Most Important Tasks

DUE   DONE

....

....

....

Other Tasks

DUE   DONE

....

....

....

....

....

....

....

....

....

....

....

....

....

NOTES

3 Most Important Tasks

DUE   DONE

....

....

....

Other Tasks

DUE   DONE

....

....

....

....

....

....

....

....

....

....

....

....

....

NOTES

BRAIN DUMP

Use this page as task triage. Write down ALL tasks rattling around in your brain and assign them a priority and a date. Transfer these tasks to your future pages as necessary then cross them out.

Tasks	PRIORITY (HIGH, MEDIUM, LOW)	ASSIGN A DATE
	○ ○ ○	
	○ ○ ○	
	○ ○ ○	
	○ ○ ○	
	○ ○ ○	
	○ ○ ○	
	○ ○ ○	
	○ ○ ○	
	○ ○ ○	
	○ ○ ○	
	○ ○ ○	
	○ ○ ○	
	○ ○ ○	
	○ ○ ○	
	○ ○ ○	
	○ ○ ○	
	○ ○ ○	
	○ ○ ○	
	○ ○ ○	
	○ ○ ○	
	○ ○ ○	
	○ ○ ○	
	○ ○ ○	
	○ ○ ○	

3 Most Important Tasks

DUE   DONE

....

....

....

Other Tasks

DUE   DONE

....

....

....

....

....

....

....

....

....

....

....

....

....

NOTES

DAY: M T W Th F S Su   DATE: _____ / _____ / _____

3 Most Important Tasks

DUE   DONE

....

....

....

Other Tasks

DUE   DONE

....

....

....

....

....

....

....

....

....

....

....

....

....

NOTES

3 Most Important Tasks

	DUE	DONE
....		☐
....		☐
....		☐

Other Tasks

	DUE	DONE
....		☐
....		☐
....		☐
....		☐
....		☐
....		☐
....		☐
....		☐
....		☐
....		☐
....		☐
....		☐
....		☐

NOTES

3 Most Important Tasks

	DUE	DONE
....	☐	☐
....	☐	☐
....	☐	☐

Other Tasks

	DUE	DONE
....	☐	☐
....	☐	☐
....	☐	☐
....	☐	☐
....	☐	☐
....	☐	☐
....	☐	☐
....	☐	☐
....	☐	☐
....	☐	☐
....	☐	☐
....	☐	☐
....	☐	☐

NOTES

3 Most Important Tasks

	DUE	DONE
....		
....		
....		

Other Tasks

	DUE	DONE
....		
....		
....		
....		
....		
....		
....		
....		
....		
....		
....		
....		
....		

NOTES

3 Most Important Tasks

	DUE	DONE
....	☐	☐
....	☐	☐
....	☐	☐

Other Tasks

	DUE	DONE
....	☐	☐
....	☐	☐
....	☐	☐
....	☐	☐
....	☐	☐
....	☐	☐
....	☐	☐
....	☐	☐
....	☐	☐
....	☐	☐
....	☐	☐
....	☐	☐
....	☐	☐

NOTES

3 Most Important Tasks

DUE   DONE

....

....

....

Other Tasks

DUE   DONE

....

....

....

....

....

....

....

....

....

....

....

....

....

NOTES

BRAIN DUMP

Use this page as task triage. Write down ALL tasks rattling around in your brain and assign them a priority and a date. Transfer these tasks to your future pages as necessary then cross them out.

Tasks

	PRIORITY (HIGH, MEDIUM, LOW)	ASSIGN A DATE
....	◯ ◯ ◯	
....	◯ ◯ ◯	
....	◯ ◯ ◯	
....	◯ ◯ ◯	
....	◯ ◯ ◯	
....	◯ ◯ ◯	
....	◯ ◯ ◯	
....	◯ ◯ ◯	
....	◯ ◯ ◯	
....	◯ ◯ ◯	
....	◯ ◯ ◯	
....	◯ ◯ ◯	
....	◯ ◯ ◯	
....	◯ ◯ ◯	
....	◯ ◯ ◯	
....	◯ ◯ ◯	
....	◯ ◯ ◯	
....	◯ ◯ ◯	
....	◯ ◯ ◯	
....	◯ ◯ ◯	
....	◯ ◯ ◯	
....	◯ ◯ ◯	
....	◯ ◯ ◯	
....	◯ ◯ ◯	

3 Most Important Tasks

DUE   DONE

....

....

....

Other Tasks

DUE   DONE

....

....

....

....

....

....

....

....

....

....

....

....

NOTES

3 Most Important Tasks

	DUE	DONE
....		☐
....		☐
....		☐

Other Tasks

	DUE	DONE
....		☐
....		☐
....		☐
....		☐
....		☐
....		☐
....		☐
....		☐
....		☐
....		☐
....		☐
....		☐
....		☐

NOTES

3 Most Important Tasks

	DUE	DONE
....	[ ]	[ ]
....	[ ]	[ ]
....	[ ]	[ ]

Other Tasks

	DUE	DONE
....	[ ]	[ ]
....	[ ]	[ ]
....	[ ]	[ ]
....	[ ]	[ ]
....	[ ]	[ ]
....	[ ]	[ ]
....	[ ]	[ ]
....	[ ]	[ ]
....	[ ]	[ ]
....	[ ]	[ ]
....	[ ]	[ ]
....	[ ]	[ ]
....	[ ]	[ ]

NOTES

3 Most Important Tasks

DUE   DONE

....

....

....

Other Tasks

DUE   DONE

....

....

....

....

....

....

....

....

....

....

....

....

....

NOTES

3 Most Important Tasks

DUE   DONE

....

....

....

Other Tasks

DUE   DONE

....

....

....

....

....

....

....

....

....

....

....

....

....

NOTES

3 Most Important Tasks

	DUE	DONE
....	☐	☐
....	☐	☐
....	☐	☐

Other Tasks

	DUE	DONE
....	☐	☐
....	☐	☐
....	☐	☐
....	☐	☐
....	☐	☐
....	☐	☐
....	☐	☐
....	☐	☐
....	☐	☐
....	☐	☐
....	☐	☐
....	☐	☐
....	☐	☐

NOTES

3 Most Important Tasks

	DUE	DONE
....		☐
....		☐
....		☐

Other Tasks

	DUE	DONE
....		☐
....		☐
....		☐
....		☐
....		☐
....		☐
....		☐
....		☐
....		☐
....		☐
....		☐
....		☐

NOTES

BRAIN DUMP

Use this page as task triage. Write down ALL tasks rattling around in your brain and assign them a priority and a date. Transfer these tasks to your future pages as necessary then cross them out.

Tasks

PRIORITY
(HIGH, MEDIUM, LOW)   ASSIGN A DATE

Task	High	Medium	Low	Date
....	○	○	○	
....	○	○	○	
....	○	○	○	
....	○	○	○	
....	○	○	○	
....	○	○	○	
....	○	○	○	
....	○	○	○	
....	○	○	○	
....	○	○	○	
....	○	○	○	
....	○	○	○	
....	○	○	○	
....	○	○	○	
....	○	○	○	
....	○	○	○	
....	○	○	○	
....	○	○	○	
....	○	○	○	
....	○	○	○	
....	○	○	○	
....	○	○	○	
....	○	○	○	
....	○	○	○	

3 Most Important Tasks

DUE   DONE

....

....

....

Other Tasks

DUE   DONE

....

....

....

....

....

....

....

....

....

....

....

....

....

NOTES

DAY: M T W Th F S Su   DATE: _____ / _____ / _____

3 Most Important Tasks

	DUE	DONE
....		
....		
....		

Other Tasks

	DUE	DONE
....		
....		
....		
....		
....		
....		
....		
....		
....		
....		
....		
....		
....		

NOTES

3 Most Important Tasks

DUE   DONE

....

....

....

Other Tasks

DUE   DONE

....

....

....

....

....

....

....

....

....

....

....

....

....

NOTES

DAY: M T W Th F S Su   DATE: _____ / _____ / _____

3 Most Important Tasks

	DUE	DONE
....		☐
....		☐
....		☐

Other Tasks

	DUE	DONE
....		☐
....		☐
....		☐
....		☐
....		☐
....		☐
....		☐
....		☐
....		☐
....		☐
....		☐
....		☐
....		☐

NOTES

3 Most Important Tasks

DUE   DONE

....

....

....

Other Tasks

DUE   DONE

....

....

....

....

....

....

....

....

....

....

....

....

....

NOTES

3 Most Important Tasks

DUE   DONE

.... ☐ ☐

.... ☐ ☐

.... ☐ ☐

Other Tasks

DUE   DONE

.... ☐ ☐

.... ☐ ☐

.... ☐ ☐

.... ☐ ☐

.... ☐ ☐

.... ☐ ☐

.... ☐ ☐

.... ☐ ☐

.... ☐ ☐

.... ☐ ☐

.... ☐ ☐

.... ☐ ☐

.... ☐ ☐

NOTES

3 Most Important Tasks

	DUE	DONE
....	☐	☐
....	☐	☐
....	☐	☐

Other Tasks

	DUE	DONE
....	☐	☐
....	☐	☐
....	☐	☐
....	☐	☐
....	☐	☐
....	☐	☐
....	☐	☐
....	☐	☐
....	☐	☐
....	☐	☐
....	☐	☐
....	☐	☐
....	☐	☐

NOTES

BRAIN DUMP

Use this page as task triage. Write down ALL tasks rattling around in your brain and assign them a priority and a date. Transfer these tasks to your future pages as necessary then cross them out.

Tasks

	PRIORITY (HIGH, MEDIUM, LOW)	ASSIGN A DATE
....	◯ ◯ ◯	
....	◯ ◯ ◯	
....	◯ ◯ ◯	
....	◯ ◯ ◯	
....	◯ ◯ ◯	
....	◯ ◯ ◯	
....	◯ ◯ ◯	
....	◯ ◯ ◯	
....	◯ ◯ ◯	
....	◯ ◯ ◯	
....	◯ ◯ ◯	
....	◯ ◯ ◯	
....	◯ ◯ ◯	
....	◯ ◯ ◯	
....	◯ ◯ ◯	
....	◯ ◯ ◯	
....	◯ ◯ ◯	
....	◯ ◯ ◯	
....	◯ ◯ ◯	
....	◯ ◯ ◯	
....	◯ ◯ ◯	
....	◯ ◯ ◯	
....	◯ ◯ ◯	

3 Most Important Tasks

	DUE	DONE
....		☐
....		☐
....		☐

Other Tasks

	DUE	DONE
....		☐
....		☐
....		☐
....		☐
....		☐
....		☐
....		☐
....		☐
....		☐
....		☐
....		☐
....		☐
....		☐

NOTES

DAY: M T W Th F S Su   DATE: _____ / _____ / _____

3 Most Important Tasks

DUE   DONE

....

....

....

Other Tasks

DUE   DONE

....

....

....

....

....

....

....

....

....

....

....

....

....

NOTES

3 Most Important Tasks

	DUE	DONE
....	☐	☐
....	☐	☐
....	☐	☐

Other Tasks

	DUE	DONE
....	☐	☐
....	☐	☐
....	☐	☐
....	☐	☐
....	☐	☐
....	☐	☐
....	☐	☐
....	☐	☐
....	☐	☐
....	☐	☐
....	☐	☐
....	☐	☐
....	☐	☐

NOTES

DAY: M T W Th F S Su   DATE: _____ / _____ / _____

3 Most Important Tasks

DUE   DONE

....

....

....

Other Tasks

DUE   DONE

....

....

....

....

....

....

....

....

....

....

....

....

....

NOTES

3 Most Important Tasks

DUE   DONE

....

....

....

Other Tasks

DUE   DONE

....

....

....

....

....

....

....

....

....

....

....

....

....

NOTES

DAY: M T W Th F S Su   DATE: _____ / _____ / _____

3 Most Important Tasks

DUE   DONE

....   ☐

....   ☐

....   ☐

Other Tasks

DUE   DONE

....   ☐

....   ☐

....   ☐

....   ☐

....   ☐

....   ☐

....   ☐

....   ☐

....   ☐

....   ☐

....   ☐

....   ☐

....   ☐

NOTES

3 Most Important Tasks

DUE   DONE

....

....

....

Other Tasks

DUE   DONE

....

....

....

....

....

....

....

....

....

....

....

....

....

NOTES

BRAIN DUMP

Use this page as task triage. Write down ALL tasks rattling around in your brain and assign them a priority and a date. Transfer these tasks to your future pages as necessary then cross them out.

Tasks

PRIORITY
(HIGH, MEDIUM, LOW)

ASSIGN A DATE

DAY: M T W Th F S Su   DATE: _____ / _____ / _____

3 Most Important Tasks

DUE   DONE

....

....

....

Other Tasks

DUE   DONE

....

....

....

....

....

....

....

....

....

....

....

....

....

NOTES

3 Most Important Tasks

DUE   DONE

....

....

....

Other Tasks

DUE   DONE

....

....

....

....

....

....

....

....

....

....

....

....

....

NOTES

3 Most Important Tasks

DUE   DONE

....

....

....

Other Tasks

DUE   DONE

....

....

....

....

....

....

....

....

....

....

....

....

....

NOTES

3 Most Important Tasks

DUE   DONE

....

....

....

Other Tasks

DUE   DONE

....

....

....

....

....

....

....

....

....

....

....

....

....

NOTES

3 Most Important Tasks

DUE   DONE

....

....

....

Other Tasks

DUE   DONE

....

....

....

....

....

....

....

....

....

....

....

....

....

NOTES

3 Most Important Tasks

DUE   DONE

....

....

....

Other Tasks

DUE   DONE

....

....

....

....

....

....

....

....

....

....

....

....

....

NOTES

3 Most Important Tasks

	DUE	DONE
....	☐	☐
....	☐	☐
....	☐	☐

Other Tasks

	DUE	DONE
....	☐	☐
....	☐	☐
....	☐	☐
....	☐	☐
....	☐	☐
....	☐	☐
....	☐	☐
....	☐	☐
....	☐	☐
....	☐	☐
....	☐	☐
....	☐	☐
....	☐	☐

NOTES

BRAIN DUMP

Use this page as task triage. Write down ALL tasks rattling around in your brain and assign them a priority and a date. Transfer these tasks to your future pages as necessary then cross them out.

Tasks

	PRIORITY (HIGH, MEDIUM, LOW)	ASSIGN A DATE
....	○ ○ ○	
....	○ ○ ○	
....	○ ○ ○	
....	○ ○ ○	
....	○ ○ ○	
....	○ ○ ○	
....	○ ○ ○	
....	○ ○ ○	
....	○ ○ ○	
....	○ ○ ○	
....	○ ○ ○	
....	○ ○ ○	
....	○ ○ ○	
....	○ ○ ○	
....	○ ○ ○	
....	○ ○ ○	
....	○ ○ ○	
....	○ ○ ○	
....	○ ○ ○	
....	○ ○ ○	
....	○ ○ ○	
....	○ ○ ○	
....	○ ○ ○	
....	○ ○ ○	
....	○ ○ ○	

3 Most Important Tasks

DUE   DONE

....

....

....

Other Tasks

DUE   DONE

....

....

....

....

....

....

....

....

....

....

....

....

....

NOTES

3 Most Important Tasks

DUE   DONE

.... ☐

.... ☐

.... ☐

Other Tasks

DUE   DONE

.... ☐

.... ☐

.... ☐

.... ☐

.... ☐

.... ☐

.... ☐

.... ☐

.... ☐

.... ☐

.... ☐

.... ☐

.... ☐

NOTES

3 Most Important Tasks

DUE   DONE

....

....

....

Other Tasks

DUE   DONE

....

....

....

....

....

....

....

....

....

....

....

....

....

NOTES

DAY: M T W Th F S Su   DATE: _____ / _____ / _____

3 Most Important Tasks

DUE   DONE

.... [   ]   [ ]

.... [   ]   [ ]

.... [   ]   [ ]

Other Tasks

DUE   DONE

.... [   ]   [ ]

.... [   ]   [ ]

.... [   ]   [ ]

.... [   ]   [ ]

.... [   ]   [ ]

.... [   ]   [ ]

.... [   ]   [ ]

.... [   ]   [ ]

.... [   ]   [ ]

.... [   ]   [ ]

.... [   ]   [ ]

.... [   ]   [ ]

.... [   ]   [ ]

NOTES

3 Most Important Tasks

DUE   DONE

....

....

....

Other Tasks

DUE   DONE

....

....

....

....

....

....

....

....

....

....

....

....

....

NOTES

DAY: M T W Th F S Su   DATE: _____ / _____ / _____

3 Most Important Tasks

	DUE	DONE
....	☐	☐
....	☐	☐
....	☐	☐

Other Tasks

	DUE	DONE
....	☐	☐
....	☐	☐
....	☐	☐
....	☐	☐
....	☐	☐
....	☐	☐
....	☐	☐
....	☐	☐
....	☐	☐
....	☐	☐
....	☐	☐
....	☐	☐
....	☐	☐

NOTES

3 Most Important Tasks

	DUE	DONE
....	☐	☐
....	☐	☐
....	☐	☐

Other Tasks

	DUE	DONE
....	☐	☐
....	☐	☐
....	☐	☐
....	☐	☐
....	☐	☐
....	☐	☐
....	☐	☐
....	☐	☐
....	☐	☐
....	☐	☐
....	☐	☐
....	☐	☐
....	☐	☐

NOTES

BRAIN DUMP

Use this page as task triage. Write down ALL tasks rattling around in your brain and assign them a priority and a date. Transfer these tasks to your future pages as necessary then cross them out.

Tasks

PRIORITY
(HIGH, MEDIUM, LOW)

ASSIGN A DATE

Tasks	High	Medium	Low	Date
....	○	○	○	
....	○	○	○	
....	○	○	○	
....	○	○	○	
....	○	○	○	
....	○	○	○	
....	○	○	○	
....	○	○	○	
....	○	○	○	
....	○	○	○	
....	○	○	○	
....	○	○	○	
....	○	○	○	
....	○	○	○	
....	○	○	○	
....	○	○	○	
....	○	○	○	
....	○	○	○	
....	○	○	○	
....	○	○	○	
....	○	○	○	
....	○	○	○	
....	○	○	○	
....	○	○	○	

3 Most Important Tasks

DUE   DONE

....

....

....

Other Tasks

DUE   DONE

....

....

....

....

....

....

....

....

....

....

....

....

....

NOTES

3 Most Important Tasks

DUE   DONE

....

....

....

Other Tasks

DUE   DONE

....

....

....

....

....

....

....

....

....

....

....

....

....

NOTES

3 Most Important Tasks

DUE   DONE

.... ☐

.... ☐

.... ☐

Other Tasks

DUE   DONE

.... ☐

.... ☐

.... ☐

.... ☐

.... ☐

.... ☐

.... ☐

.... ☐

.... ☐

.... ☐

.... ☐

.... ☐

.... ☐

NOTES

3 Most Important Tasks

DUE   DONE

....

....

....

Other Tasks

DUE   DONE

....

....

....

....

....

....

....

....

....

....

....

....

....

NOTES

3 Most Important Tasks

                                                                    DUE   DONE

....   [   ]   [ ]

....   [   ]   [ ]

....   [   ]   [ ]

Other Tasks

                                                                    DUE   DONE

....   [   ]   [ ]

....   [   ]   [ ]

....   [   ]   [ ]

....   [   ]   [ ]

....   [   ]   [ ]

....   [   ]   [ ]

....   [   ]   [ ]

....   [   ]   [ ]

....   [   ]   [ ]

....   [   ]   [ ]

....   [   ]   [ ]

....   [   ]   [ ]

....   [   ]   [ ]

NOTES

3 Most Important Tasks

	DUE	DONE
....	☐	☐
....	☐	☐
....	☐	☐

Other Tasks

	DUE	DONE
....	☐	☐
....	☐	☐
....	☐	☐
....	☐	☐
....	☐	☐
....	☐	☐
....	☐	☐
....	☐	☐
....	☐	☐
....	☐	☐
....	☐	☐
....	☐	☐
....	☐	☐

NOTES

3 Most Important Tasks

DUE   DONE

.... ☐

.... ☐

.... ☐

Other Tasks

DUE   DONE

.... ☐

.... ☐

.... ☐

.... ☐

.... ☐

.... ☐

.... ☐

.... ☐

.... ☐

.... ☐

.... ☐

.... ☐

.... ☐

NOTES

BRAIN DUMP

Use this page as task triage. Write down ALL tasks rattling around in your brain and assign them a priority and a date. Transfer these tasks to your future pages as necessary then cross them out.

Tasks

PRIORITY
(HIGH, MEDIUM, LOW)

ASSIGN A DATE

3 Most Important Tasks

DUE   DONE

....

....

....

Other Tasks

DUE   DONE

....

....

....

....

....

....

....

....

....

....

....

....

....

NOTES

3 Most Important Tasks

	DUE	DONE
....		☐
....		☐
....		☐

Other Tasks

	DUE	DONE
....		☐
....		☐
....		☐
....		☐
....		☐
....		☐
....		☐
....		☐
....		☐
....		☐
....		☐
....		☐
....		☐

NOTES

3 Most Important Tasks

DUE   DONE

....

....

....

Other Tasks

DUE   DONE

....

....

....

....

....

....

....

....

....

....

....

....

....

NOTES

3 Most Important Tasks

DUE   DONE

....

....

....

Other Tasks

DUE   DONE

....

....

....

....

....

....

....

....

....

....

....

....

....

NOTES

DAY: M T W Th F S Su   DATE: _____/_____/_____

3 Most Important Tasks

DUE   DONE

....

....

....

Other Tasks

DUE   DONE

....

....

....

....

....

....

....

....

....

....

....

....

NOTES

DAY: M T W Th F S Su   DATE: _____ / _____ / _____

3 Most Important Tasks

	DUE	DONE
....		
....		
....		

Other Tasks

	DUE	DONE
....		
....		
....		
....		
....		
....		
....		
....		
....		
....		
....		
....		
....		

NOTES

3 Most Important Tasks

DUE   DONE

....

....

....

Other Tasks

DUE   DONE

....

....

....

....

....

....

....

....

....

....

....

....

....

NOTES

BRAIN DUMP

Use this page as task triage. Write down ALL tasks rattling around in your brain and assign them a priority and a date. Transfer these tasks to your future pages as necessary then cross them out.

Tasks	PRIORITY (HIGH, MEDIUM, LOW)			ASSIGN A DATE
	○	○	○	
	○	○	○	
	○	○	○	
	○	○	○	
	○	○	○	
	○	○	○	
	○	○	○	
	○	○	○	
	○	○	○	
	○	○	○	
	○	○	○	
	○	○	○	
	○	○	○	
	○	○	○	
	○	○	○	
	○	○	○	
	○	○	○	
	○	○	○	
	○	○	○	
	○	○	○	
	○	○	○	
	○	○	○	
	○	○	○	
	○	○	○	

3 Most Important Tasks

DUE   DONE

....

....

....

Other Tasks

DUE   DONE

....

....

....

....

....

....

....

....

....

....

....

....

....

NOTES

DAY: M T W Th F S Su   DATE: _____ / _____ / _____

3 Most Important Tasks

DUE   DONE

....

....

....

Other Tasks

DUE   DONE

....

....

....

....

....

....

....

....

....

....

....

....

....

NOTES

3 Most Important Tasks

	DUE	DONE
....	☐	☐
....	☐	☐
....	☐	☐

Other Tasks

	DUE	DONE
....	☐	☐
....	☐	☐
....	☐	☐
....	☐	☐
....	☐	☐
....	☐	☐
....	☐	☐
....	☐	☐
....	☐	☐
....	☐	☐
....	☐	☐
....	☐	☐
....	☐	☐

NOTES

3 Most Important Tasks

DUE   DONE

....

....

....

Other Tasks

DUE   DONE

....

....

....

....

....

....

....

....

....

....

....

....

....

NOTES

3 Most Important Tasks

	DUE	DONE
....	☐	☐
....	☐	☐
....	☐	☐

Other Tasks

	DUE	DONE
....	☐	☐
....	☐	☐
....	☐	☐
....	☐	☐
....	☐	☐
....	☐	☐
....	☐	☐
....	☐	☐
....	☐	☐
....	☐	☐
....	☐	☐
....	☐	☐
....	☐	☐

NOTES

DAY: M T W Th F S Su   DATE: _____ / _____ / _____

3 Most Important Tasks

DUE   DONE

....   ☐

....   ☐

....   ☐

Other Tasks

DUE   DONE

....   ☐

....   ☐

....   ☐

....   ☐

....   ☐

....   ☐

....   ☐

....   ☐

....   ☐

....   ☐

....   ☐

....   ☐

....   ☐

NOTES

3 Most Important Tasks

DUE   DONE

....

....

....

Other Tasks

DUE   DONE

....

....

....

....

....

....

....

....

....

....

....

....

....

NOTES

BRAIN DUMP

Use this page as task triage. Write down ALL tasks rattling around in your brain and assign them a priority and a date. Transfer these tasks to your future pages as necessary then cross them out.

Tasks

PRIORITY
(HIGH, MEDIUM, LOW)

ASSIGN A DATE

3 Most Important Tasks

DUE   DONE

···

···

···

Other Tasks

DUE   DONE

···

···

···

···

···

···

···

···

···

···

···

···

···

NOTES

DAY: M T W Th F S Su   DATE: _____ / _____ / _____

3 Most Important Tasks

DUE   DONE

....   ☐

....   ☐

....   ☐

Other Tasks

DUE   DONE

....   ☐

....   ☐

....   ☐

....   ☐

....   ☐

....   ☐

....   ☐

....   ☐

....   ☐

....   ☐

....   ☐

....   ☐

....   ☐

NOTES

3 Most Important Tasks

DUE   DONE

....

....

....

Other Tasks

DUE   DONE

....

....

....

....

....

....

....

....

....

....

....

....

....

NOTES

3 Most Important Tasks

DUE   DONE

....

....

....

Other Tasks

DUE   DONE

....

....

....

....

....

....

....

....

....

....

....

....

....

NOTES

3 Most Important Tasks

DUE   DONE

....

....

....

Other Tasks

DUE   DONE

....

....

....

....

....

....

....

....

....

....

....

....

NOTES

DAY: M T W Th F S Su   DATE: _____ / _____ / _____

3 Most Important Tasks

DUE   DONE

....

....

....

Other Tasks

DUE   DONE

....

....

....

....

....

....

....

....

....

....

....

....

NOTES

3 Most Important Tasks

	DUE	DONE
....	☐	☐
....	☐	☐
....	☐	☐

Other Tasks

	DUE	DONE
....	☐	☐
....	☐	☐
....	☐	☐
....	☐	☐
....	☐	☐
....	☐	☐
....	☐	☐
....	☐	☐
....	☐	☐
....	☐	☐
....	☐	☐
....	☐	☐
....	☐	☐

NOTES

BRAIN DUMP

Use this page as task triage. Write down ALL tasks rattling around in your brain and assign them a priority and a date. Transfer these tasks to your future pages as necessary then cross them out.

Tasks	PRIORITY (HIGH, MEDIUM, LOW)	ASSIGN A DATE
	○ ○ ○	
	○ ○ ○	
	○ ○ ○	
	○ ○ ○	
	○ ○ ○	
	○ ○ ○	
	○ ○ ○	
	○ ○ ○	
	○ ○ ○	
	○ ○ ○	
	○ ○ ○	
	○ ○ ○	
	○ ○ ○	
	○ ○ ○	
	○ ○ ○	
	○ ○ ○	
	○ ○ ○	
	○ ○ ○	
	○ ○ ○	
	○ ○ ○	
	○ ○ ○	
	○ ○ ○	
	○ ○ ○	

3 Most Important Tasks

DUE   DONE

....

....

....

Other Tasks

DUE   DONE

....

....

....

....

....

....

....

....

....

....

....

....

....

NOTES

DAY: M T W Th F S Su   DATE: _____ / _____ / _____

3 Most Important Tasks

DUE   DONE

....

....

....

Other Tasks

DUE   DONE

....

....

....

....

....

....

....

....

....

....

....

....

....

NOTES

3 Most Important Tasks

DUE   DONE

....

....

....

Other Tasks

DUE   DONE

....

....

....

....

....

....

....

....

....

....

....

....

....

NOTES

3 Most Important Tasks

DUE   DONE

....

....

....

Other Tasks

DUE   DONE

....

....

....

....

....

....

....

....

....

....

....

....

....

NOTES

3 Most Important Tasks

	DUE	DONE
....		☐
....		☐
....		☐

Other Tasks

	DUE	DONE
....		☐
....		☐
....		☐
....		☐
....		☐
....		☐
....		☐
....		☐
....		☐
....		☐
....		☐
....		☐
....		☐

NOTES

3 Most Important Tasks

DUE   DONE

....

....

....

Other Tasks

DUE   DONE

....

....

....

....

....

....

....

....

....

....

....

....

....

NOTES

3 Most Important Tasks

DUE   DONE

....

....

....

Other Tasks

DUE   DONE

....

....

....

....

....

....

....

....

....

....

....

....

....

NOTES

BRAIN DUMP

Use this page as task triage. Write down ALL tasks rattling around in your brain and assign them a priority and a date. Transfer these tasks to your future pages as necessary then cross them out.

Tasks

	PRIORITY (HIGH, MEDIUM, LOW)	ASSIGN A DATE
....	◯ ◯ ◯	
....	◯ ◯ ◯	
....	◯ ◯ ◯	
....	◯ ◯ ◯	
....	◯ ◯ ◯	
....	◯ ◯ ◯	
....	◯ ◯ ◯	
....	◯ ◯ ◯	
....	◯ ◯ ◯	
....	◯ ◯ ◯	
....	◯ ◯ ◯	
....	◯ ◯ ◯	
....	◯ ◯ ◯	
....	◯ ◯ ◯	
....	◯ ◯ ◯	
....	◯ ◯ ◯	
....	◯ ◯ ◯	
....	◯ ◯ ◯	
....	◯ ◯ ◯	
....	◯ ◯ ◯	
....	◯ ◯ ◯	
....	◯ ◯ ◯	
....	◯ ◯ ◯	
....	◯ ◯ ◯	

3 Most Important Tasks

DUE   DONE

....

....

....

Other Tasks

DUE   DONE

....

....

....

....

....

....

....

....

....

....

....

....

NOTES

3 Most Important Tasks

	DUE	DONE
....		
....		
....		

Other Tasks

	DUE	DONE
....		
....		
....		
....		
....		
....		
....		
....		
....		
....		
....		
....		
....		

NOTES

3 Most Important Tasks

DUE   DONE

....

....

....

Other Tasks

DUE   DONE

....

....

....

....

....

....

....

....

....

....

....

....

....

NOTES

DAY: M T W Th F S Su   DATE: _____ / _____ / _____

3 Most Important Tasks

DUE   DONE

....   ☐

....   ☐

....   ☐

Other Tasks

DUE   DONE

....   ☐

....   ☐

....   ☐

....   ☐

....   ☐

....   ☐

....   ☐

....   ☐

....   ☐

....   ☐

....   ☐

....   ☐

....   ☐

NOTES

DAY: M T W Th F S Su   DATE: _____ / _____ / _____

3 Most Important Tasks

DUE   DONE

....   [ ]   [ ]

....   [ ]   [ ]

....   [ ]   [ ]

Other Tasks

DUE   DONE

....   [ ]   [ ]

....   [ ]   [ ]

....   [ ]   [ ]

....   [ ]   [ ]

....   [ ]   [ ]

....   [ ]   [ ]

....   [ ]   [ ]

....   [ ]   [ ]

....   [ ]   [ ]

....   [ ]   [ ]

....   [ ]   [ ]

....   [ ]   [ ]

....   [ ]   [ ]

NOTES

3 Most Important Tasks

	DUE	DONE
....		☐
....		☐
....		☐

Other Tasks

	DUE	DONE
....		☐
....		☐
....		☐
....		☐
....		☐
....		☐
....		☐
....		☐
....		☐
....		☐
....		☐
....		☐
....		☐

NOTES

3 Most Important Tasks

DUE   DONE

....

....

....

Other Tasks

DUE   DONE

....

....

....

....

....

....

....

....

....

....

....

....

....

NOTES

BRAIN DUMP

Use this page as task triage. Write down ALL tasks rattling around in your brain and assign them a priority and a date. Transfer these tasks to your future pages as necessary then cross them out.

Tasks

PRIORITY
(HIGH, MEDIUM, LOW)   ASSIGN A DATE

Tasks	Priority			Assign a Date
....	○	○	○	
....	○	○	○	
....	○	○	○	
....	○	○	○	
....	○	○	○	
....	○	○	○	
....	○	○	○	
....	○	○	○	
....	○	○	○	
....	○	○	○	
....	○	○	○	
....	○	○	○	
....	○	○	○	
....	○	○	○	
....	○	○	○	
....	○	○	○	
....	○	○	○	
....	○	○	○	
....	○	○	○	
....	○	○	○	
....	○	○	○	
....	○	○	○	
....	○	○	○	
....	○	○	○	

3 Most Important Tasks

	DUE	DONE
....	☐	☐
....	☐	☐
....	☐	☐

Other Tasks

	DUE	DONE
....	☐	☐
....	☐	☐
....	☐	☐
....	☐	☐
....	☐	☐
....	☐	☐
....	☐	☐
....	☐	☐
....	☐	☐
....	☐	☐
....	☐	☐
....	☐	☐
....	☐	☐

NOTES

3 Most Important Tasks

DUE   DONE

....

....

....

Other Tasks

DUE   DONE

....

....

....

....

....

....

....

....

....

....

....

....

....

NOTES

3 Most Important Tasks

	DUE	DONE
....	☐	☐
....	☐	☐
....	☐	☐

Other Tasks

	DUE	DONE
....	☐	☐
....	☐	☐
....	☐	☐
....	☐	☐
....	☐	☐
....	☐	☐
....	☐	☐
....	☐	☐
....	☐	☐
....	☐	☐
....	☐	☐
....	☐	☐
....	☐	☐

NOTES

3 Most Important Tasks

DUE   DONE

....

....

....

Other Tasks

DUE   DONE

....

....

....

....

....

....

....

....

....

....

....

....

NOTES

3 Most Important Tasks

DUE   DONE

....

....

....

Other Tasks

DUE   DONE

....

....

....

....

....

....

....

....

....

....

....

....

....

NOTES

3 Most Important Tasks

DUE   DONE

....

....

....

Other Tasks

DUE   DONE

....

....

....

....

....

....

....

....

....

....

....

....

....

NOTES

3 Most Important Tasks

DUE   DONE

....

....

....

Other Tasks

DUE   DONE

....

....

....

....

....

....

....

....

....

....

....

....

....

NOTES

BRAIN DUMP

Use this page as task triage. Write down ALL tasks rattling around in your brain and assign them a priority and a date. Transfer these tasks to your future pages as necessary then cross them out.

Tasks

<table>
<tr><td>Tasks</td><td colspan="3">PRIORITY
(HIGH, MEDIUM, LOW)</td><td>ASSIGN A DATE</td></tr>
<tr><td>..</td><td>○</td><td>○</td><td>○</td><td></td></tr>
<tr><td>..</td><td>○</td><td>○</td><td>○</td><td></td></tr>
<tr><td>..</td><td>○</td><td>○</td><td>○</td><td></td></tr>
<tr><td>..</td><td>○</td><td>○</td><td>○</td><td></td></tr>
<tr><td>..</td><td>○</td><td>○</td><td>○</td><td></td></tr>
<tr><td>..</td><td>○</td><td>○</td><td>○</td><td></td></tr>
<tr><td>..</td><td>○</td><td>○</td><td>○</td><td></td></tr>
<tr><td>..</td><td>○</td><td>○</td><td>○</td><td></td></tr>
<tr><td>..</td><td>○</td><td>○</td><td>○</td><td></td></tr>
<tr><td>..</td><td>○</td><td>○</td><td>○</td><td></td></tr>
<tr><td>..</td><td>○</td><td>○</td><td>○</td><td></td></tr>
<tr><td>..</td><td>○</td><td>○</td><td>○</td><td></td></tr>
<tr><td>..</td><td>○</td><td>○</td><td>○</td><td></td></tr>
<tr><td>..</td><td>○</td><td>○</td><td>○</td><td></td></tr>
<tr><td>..</td><td>○</td><td>○</td><td>○</td><td></td></tr>
<tr><td>..</td><td>○</td><td>○</td><td>○</td><td></td></tr>
<tr><td>..</td><td>○</td><td>○</td><td>○</td><td></td></tr>
<tr><td>..</td><td>○</td><td>○</td><td>○</td><td></td></tr>
<tr><td>..</td><td>○</td><td>○</td><td>○</td><td></td></tr>
<tr><td>..</td><td>○</td><td>○</td><td>○</td><td></td></tr>
<tr><td>..</td><td>○</td><td>○</td><td>○</td><td></td></tr>
<tr><td>..</td><td>○</td><td>○</td><td>○</td><td></td></tr>
<tr><td>..</td><td>○</td><td>○</td><td>○</td><td></td></tr>
<tr><td>..</td><td>○</td><td>○</td><td>○</td><td></td></tr>
</table>

3 Most Important Tasks

DUE   DONE

....

....

....

Other Tasks

DUE   DONE

....

....

....

....

....

....

....

....

....

....

....

....

....

NOTES

DAY: M T W Th F S Su   DATE: _____ / _____ / _____

3 Most Important Tasks

DUE   DONE

....   [   ]   [   ]

....   [   ]   [   ]

....   [   ]   [   ]

Other Tasks

DUE   DONE

....   [   ]   [   ]

....   [   ]   [   ]

....   [   ]   [   ]

....   [   ]   [   ]

....   [   ]   [   ]

....   [   ]   [   ]

....   [   ]   [   ]

....   [   ]   [   ]

....   [   ]   [   ]

....   [   ]   [   ]

....   [   ]   [   ]

....   [   ]   [   ]

....   [   ]   [   ]

NOTES

3 Most Important Tasks

DUE   DONE

....

....

....

Other Tasks

DUE   DONE

....

....

....

....

....

....

....

....

....

....

....

....

....

NOTES

3 Most Important Tasks

DUE　　DONE

....

....

....

Other Tasks

DUE　　DONE

....

....

....

....

....

....

....

....

....

....

....

....

....

NOTES

DAY: M T W Th F S Su   DATE: _____ / _____ / _____

3 Most Important Tasks

                                                              DUE   DONE

.... [   ]   [ ]

.... [   ]   [ ]

.... [   ]   [ ]

Other Tasks

                                                              DUE   DONE

.... [   ]   [ ]

.... [   ]   [ ]

.... [   ]   [ ]

.... [   ]   [ ]

.... [   ]   [ ]

.... [   ]   [ ]

.... [   ]   [ ]

.... [   ]   [ ]

.... [   ]   [ ]

.... [   ]   [ ]

.... [   ]   [ ]

.... [   ]   [ ]

.... [   ]   [ ]

NOTES

DAY: M T W Th F S Su   DATE: _____ / _____ / _____

3 Most Important Tasks

DUE   DONE

....

....

....

Other Tasks

DUE   DONE

....

....

....

....

....

....

....

....

....

....

....

....

....

NOTES

3 Most Important Tasks

	DUE	DONE
....	☐	☐
....	☐	☐
....	☐	☐

Other Tasks

	DUE	DONE
....	☐	☐
....	☐	☐
....	☐	☐
....	☐	☐
....	☐	☐
....	☐	☐
....	☐	☐
....	☐	☐
....	☐	☐
....	☐	☐
....	☐	☐
....	☐	☐
....	☐	☐

NOTES

BRAIN DUMP

Use this page as task triage. Write down ALL tasks rattling around in your brain and assign them a priority and a date. Transfer these tasks to your future pages as necessary then cross them out.

Tasks

	PRIORITY (HIGH, MEDIUM, LOW)			ASSIGN A DATE
....	○	○	○	
....	○	○	○	
....	○	○	○	
....	○	○	○	
....	○	○	○	
....	○	○	○	
....	○	○	○	
....	○	○	○	
....	○	○	○	
....	○	○	○	
....	○	○	○	
....	○	○	○	
....	○	○	○	
....	○	○	○	
....	○	○	○	
....	○	○	○	
....	○	○	○	
....	○	○	○	
....	○	○	○	
....	○	○	○	
....	○	○	○	
....	○	○	○	
....	○	○	○	

3 Most Important Tasks

DUE   DONE

....

....

....

Other Tasks

DUE   DONE

....

....

....

....

....

....

....

....

....

....

....

....

....

NOTES

3 Most Important Tasks

DUE   DONE

....

....

....

Other Tasks

DUE   DONE

....

....

....

....

....

....

....

....

....

....

....

....

....

NOTES

3 Most Important Tasks

DUE   DONE

....

....

....

Other Tasks

DUE   DONE

....

....

....

....

....

....

....

....

....

....

....

....

....

NOTES

3 Most Important Tasks

DUE   DONE

....

....

....

Other Tasks

DUE   DONE

....

....

....

....

....

....

....

....

....

....

....

....

....

NOTES

3 Most Important Tasks

DUE   DONE

....

....

....

Other Tasks

DUE   DONE

....

....

....

....

....

....

....

....

....

....

....

....

....

NOTES

3 Most Important Tasks

DUE   DONE

....

....

....

Other Tasks

DUE   DONE

....

....

....

....

....

....

....

....

....

....

....

....

....

NOTES

3 Most Important Tasks

DUE   DONE

....

....

....

Other Tasks

DUE   DONE

....

....

....

....

....

....

....

....

....

....

....

....

....

NOTES

BRAIN DUMP

Use this page as task triage. Write down ALL tasks rattling around in your brain and assign them a priority and a date. Transfer these tasks to your future pages as necessary then cross them out.

Tasks

PRIORITY
(HIGH, MEDIUM, LOW)

ASSIGN A DATE

Tasks	High	Medium	Low	Date
....	○	○	○	
....	○	○	○	
....	○	○	○	
....	○	○	○	
....	○	○	○	
....	○	○	○	
....	○	○	○	
....	○	○	○	
....	○	○	○	
....	○	○	○	
....	○	○	○	
....	○	○	○	
....	○	○	○	
....	○	○	○	
....	○	○	○	
....	○	○	○	
....	○	○	○	
....	○	○	○	
....	○	○	○	
....	○	○	○	
....	○	○	○	
....	○	○	○	
....	○	○	○	
....	○	○	○	

3 Most Important Tasks

DUE   DONE

....

....

....

Other Tasks

DUE   DONE

....

....

....

....

....

....

....

....

....

....

....

....

....

NOTES

3 Most Important Tasks

DUE DONE

....

....

....

Other Tasks

DUE DONE

....

....

....

....

....

....

....

....

....

....

....

....

....

NOTES

3 Most Important Tasks

DUE   DONE

....

....

....

Other Tasks

DUE   DONE

....

....

....

....

....

....

....

....

....

....

....

....

NOTES

3 Most Important Tasks

DUE   DONE

....

....

....

Other Tasks

DUE   DONE

....

....

....

....

....

....

....

....

....

....

....

....

....

NOTES

DAY: M T W Th F S Su   DATE: _____ / _____ / _____

3 Most Important Tasks

DUE   DONE

....

....

....

Other Tasks

DUE   DONE

....

....

....

....

....

....

....

....

....

....

....

....

....

NOTES

DAY: M T W Th F S Su   DATE: _____ / _____ / _____

3 Most Important Tasks

DUE   DONE

....

....

....

Other Tasks

DUE   DONE

....

....

....

....

....

....

....

....

....

....

....

....

....

NOTES

3 Most Important Tasks

DUE   DONE

....

....

....

Other Tasks

DUE   DONE

....

....

....

....

....

....

....

....

....

....

....

....

....

NOTES

BRAIN DUMP

Use this page as task triage. Write down ALL tasks rattling around in your brain and assign them a priority and a date. Transfer these tasks to your future pages as necessary then cross them out.

Tasks	PRIORITY (HIGH, MEDIUM, LOW)			ASSIGN A DATE
....	◯	◯	◯	
....	◯	◯	◯	
....	◯	◯	◯	
....	◯	◯	◯	
....	◯	◯	◯	
....	◯	◯	◯	
....	◯	◯	◯	
....	◯	◯	◯	
....	◯	◯	◯	
....	◯	◯	◯	
....	◯	◯	◯	
....	◯	◯	◯	
....	◯	◯	◯	
....	◯	◯	◯	
....	◯	◯	◯	
....	◯	◯	◯	
....	◯	◯	◯	
....	◯	◯	◯	
....	◯	◯	◯	
....	◯	◯	◯	
....	◯	◯	◯	
....	◯	◯	◯	
....	◯	◯	◯	
....	◯	◯	◯	

DAY: M T W Th F S Su   DATE: _____ / _____ / _____

3 Most Important Tasks

DUE   DONE

....   ☐

....   ☐

....   ☐

Other Tasks

DUE   DONE

....   ☐

....   ☐

....   ☐

....   ☐

....   ☐

....   ☐

....   ☐

....   ☐

....   ☐

....   ☐

....   ☐

....   ☐

....   ☐

NOTES

DAY: M T W Th F S Su   DATE: _____ / _____ / _____

3 Most Important Tasks

                                                    DUE   DONE

....

....

....

Other Tasks

                                                    DUE   DONE

....

....

....

....

....

....

....

....

....

....

....

....

....

NOTES

3 Most Important Tasks

DUE   DONE

....

....

....

Other Tasks

DUE   DONE

....

....

....

....

....

....

....

....

....

....

....

....

....

NOTES

DAY: M T W Th F S Su   DATE: _____ / _____ / _____

3 Most Important Tasks

DUE   DONE

.... ☐

.... ☐

.... ☐

Other Tasks

DUE   DONE

.... ☐

.... ☐

.... ☐

.... ☐

.... ☐

.... ☐

.... ☐

.... ☐

.... ☐

.... ☐

.... ☐

.... ☐

.... ☐

NOTES

DAY: M T W Th F S Su   DATE: _____ / _____ / _____

3 Most Important Tasks

	DUE	DONE
....		
....		
....		

Other Tasks

	DUE	DONE
....		
....		
....		
....		
....		
....		
....		
....		
....		
....		
....		
....		
....		

NOTES

3 Most Important Tasks

DUE   DONE

....

....

....

Other Tasks

DUE   DONE

....

....

....

....

....

....

....

....

....

....

....

....

NOTES

3 Most Important Tasks

	DUE	DONE
....		
....		
....		

Other Tasks

	DUE	DONE
....		
....		
....		
....		
....		
....		
....		
....		
....		
....		
....		
....		
....		

NOTES

BRAIN DUMP

Use this page as task triage. Write down ALL tasks rattling around in your brain and assign them a priority and a date. Transfer these tasks to your future pages as necessary then cross them out.

Tasks	PRIORITY (HIGH, MEDIUM, LOW)			ASSIGN A DATE
....	○	○	○	
....	○	○	○	
....	○	○	○	
....	○	○	○	
....	○	○	○	
....	○	○	○	
....	○	○	○	
....	○	○	○	
....	○	○	○	
....	○	○	○	
....	○	○	○	
....	○	○	○	
....	○	○	○	
....	○	○	○	
....	○	○	○	
....	○	○	○	
....	○	○	○	
....	○	○	○	
....	○	○	○	
....	○	○	○	
....	○	○	○	
....	○	○	○	
....	○	○	○	
....	○	○	○	

3 Most Important Tasks

	DUE	DONE
....	☐	☐
....	☐	☐
....	☐	☐

Other Tasks

	DUE	DONE
....	☐	☐
....	☐	☐
....	☐	☐
....	☐	☐
....	☐	☐
....	☐	☐
....	☐	☐
....	☐	☐
....	☐	☐
....	☐	☐
....	☐	☐
....	☐	☐

NOTES

DAY: M T W Th F S Su   DATE: _____ / _____ / _____

3 Most Important Tasks

	DUE	DONE
....		☐
....		☐
....		☐

Other Tasks

	DUE	DONE
....		☐
....		☐
....		☐
....		☐
....		☐
....		☐
....		☐
....		☐
....		☐
....		☐
....		☐
....		☐
....		☐

NOTES

3 Most Important Tasks

DUE   DONE

....

....

....

Other Tasks

DUE   DONE

....

....

....

....

....

....

....

....

....

....

....

....

....

NOTES

3 Most Important Tasks

DUE   DONE

....

....

....

Other Tasks

DUE   DONE

....

....

....

....

....

....

....

....

....

....

....

....

....

NOTES

3 Most Important Tasks

DUE   DONE

....

....

....

Other Tasks

DUE   DONE

....

....

....

....

....

....

....

....

....

....

....

....

....

NOTES

DAY: M T W Th F S Su   DATE: _____ / _____ / _____

3 Most Important Tasks

DUE   DONE

....

....

....

Other Tasks

DUE   DONE

....

....

....

....

....

....

....

....

....

....

....

....

....

NOTES

3 Most Important Tasks

DUE   DONE

....

....

....

Other Tasks

DUE   DONE

....

....

....

....

....

....

....

....

....

....

....

....

NOTES

BRAIN DUMP

Use this page as task triage. Write down ALL tasks rattling around in your brain and assign them a priority and a date. Transfer these tasks to your future pages as necessary then cross them out.

Tasks

ASSIGN A DATE

Tasks	Priority	Assign a Date
....	○ ○ ○	
....	○ ○ ○	
....	○ ○ ○	
....	○ ○ ○	
....	○ ○ ○	
....	○ ○ ○	
....	○ ○ ○	
....	○ ○ ○	
....	○ ○ ○	
....	○ ○ ○	
....	○ ○ ○	
....	○ ○ ○	
....	○ ○ ○	
....	○ ○ ○	
....	○ ○ ○	
....	○ ○ ○	
....	○ ○ ○	
....	○ ○ ○	
....	○ ○ ○	
....	○ ○ ○	
....	○ ○ ○	
....	○ ○ ○	
....	○ ○ ○	
....	○ ○ ○	

3 Most Important Tasks

DUE   DONE

....

....

....

Other Tasks

DUE   DONE

....

....

....

....

....

....

....

....

....

....

....

....

NOTES

DAY: M T W Th F S Su   DATE: _____ / _____ / _____

3 Most Important Tasks

	DUE	DONE
....		☐
....		☐
....		☐

Other Tasks

	DUE	DONE
....		☐
....		☐
....		☐
....		☐
....		☐
....		☐
....		☐
....		☐
....		☐
....		☐
....		☐
....		☐
....		☐

NOTES

3 Most Important Tasks

DUE   DONE

....

....

....

Other Tasks

DUE   DONE

....

....

....

....

....

....

....

....

....

....

....

....

NOTES

Made in the USA
Middletown, DE
26 January 2021